MW01141677

GENERATION J

GENERATION J

25 Gospel Meditations on Life and Vocation

Santos G. Mena, SJ

Saint Mary's Press®

Genuine recycled paper with 10% post-consumer waste.
51088

All Scripture quotations in this publication are from the Good
News Translation, Second Edition. Copyright © 1992 by
American Bible Society. Used by permission.

Originally published as *The J Team* by the Cardinal Bea Institute, Ateneo
de Manila University.

New edition published by The Jesuit Communications Foundation, Inc.

Published in the United States by Saint Mary's Press, Christian Brothers
Publications, 702 Terrace Heights, Winona, MN 55987-1318,
www.smp.org.

The Saint Mary's Press publishing team included John Vitek, develop-
ment editor; prepress and manufacturing coordinated by the pre-
publication and production services departments of Saint Mary's Press.

ISBN 0-88489-901-2

Library of Congress Cataloging-in-Publication Data

Mena, Santos G.
[Team]
Generation J : 25 gospel meditations on life and vocation / Santos
G. Mena.
p. cm.
ISBN 0-88489-901-2 (pbk.)
1. Youth—Religious life. 2. Youth—Prayer-books and devotions—
English. 3. Bible. N.T. Gospels—Meditations. I. Title.
BV4531.3. M45 2005
242'.93—dc22

2005002520

To you, young men and women,
whom the love of Christ
impels to ever higher levels
of generosity.

CONTENTS

Wow! 9

1   Why Me? 12

2   Unusually Lucky 18

3   Take Aim 22

4   The Dreamer 27

5   The Loafer 31

6   Business as Usual 35

7   Are Stars Really Unreachable? 38

8   See No Evil 43

9   Hear No Evil, Speak No Evil 47

10   Thirsty? 51

11 Be Guided 56

12 Up and About 61

13 Deep Freeze 65

14 A Surprise Attack 73

15 Up a Tree 79

16 Give and Take 84

17 Three's Company 90

18 The Goody-Goody Too 94

19 The Name of the Game: Part One 98

20 The Name of the Game: Part Two 102

21 The Name of the Game: Part Three 106

22 The Cost: Part One 109

23 The Cost: Part Two 114

24 Johnny . . . What's His Name? 120

25 A Bumper Crop 125

Biblical Index 128

WOW!

So what if God is calling you?

Priesthood or religious life has suddenly become a real possibility for you.

And so, you feel like wondering.

Yes, you are invited to think.

And to reflect.

And if while doing that, you feel sort of thrilled — well, go ahead and enjoy that thrill.

Be thrilled, my friend.

Allow the idea to seize you.

That is precisely the nature of a call, of a vocation: it seizes, it thrills, it makes the heart beat faster.

And it fills the mind with a sense of wonder.

It leads you to ask yourself: "Really? Is it possible? Is God calling me? Has God some plans for me?"

For me? Wow!

Yes, you're right: Wow!

I think all of us who have felt the call have, at one time or another, also exclaimed, "Wow!"

Now, watch it, my friend.

It's fair I inform you that you might be already getting into it.

If you have said to yourself, "Wow!" and have at the same time felt a gentle, sweet gnawing in your heart, this could be the first of a series of green lights that may signal a traffic-free highway ahead of you.

In other words . . .

This simple "Wow!" could already be the first positive sign of a vocation.

Wow!

So, if you are courageous enough, go on and proceed to explore.

Go on and pray to encounter many more green lights.

Only green lights.

For God could be waiting for you at the end of the freeway.

Unless . . .

Unless you develop cold feet, use a temporary red light, a temporary setback, a flat tire or something, and give up the idea.

Unless . . .

Unless you suddenly see one of the many exits along the way, and on an impulse, decide to ease yourself off the highway and forget your quest.

(Wow . . .)

———————

The following reflections are devised to help you see things more clearly.

For only if you see things clearly can you decide intelligently.

No, do not be afraid to go through this book.

If you don't have a vocation from God, this book won't give you one.

Only Jesus can rope you in.

For all you know, this book could confirm that you do not have a vocation.

You will have achieved at least this: the assurance that you do not have it.

Now, did you notice the word I used a few lines back?

I wrote *reflections*.

Don't just read these meditations.

For these pages are like chewing gum; they are to be chewed.

And relished.

And turned over and over for as long as they yield some flavor.

It would be foolish for you to swallow a piece of chewing gum straight.

It would also be foolish if you just read these pages.

And I am sure you aren't foolish.

For this book is not to be read, not to be swallowed the way a turkey gobbles a food pellet.

This book is to be reflected upon, to be chewed, again and again, in the intimacy of your heart with Jesus.

In other words, this book is to be prayed upon.

WHY ME?

After this, Jesus went across Lake Galilee (or Lake Tiberias, as it is also called). A large crowd followed him, because they had seen his miracles of healing the sick. Jesus went up a hill and sat down with his disciples. The time for the Passover Festival was near. Jesus looked around and saw that a large crowd was coming to him, so he asked Philip, "Where can we buy enough food to feed all these people?" (He said this to test Philip; actually he already knew what he would do.)

Philip answered, "For everyone to have even a little, it would take more than two hundred silver coins to buy enough bread."

Another one of this disciples, Andrew, who was Simon Peter's brother, said, "There is a boy here who has five loaves of barley bread and two fish. But they will certainly not be enough for all these people."

"Make the people sit down," Jesus told them. (There was a lot of grass there.) So all the people sat down; there were about five thousand men. Jesus took the bread, gave thanks to God, and distributed it to the people who were sitting there. He did the

same with the fish, and they all had as much as
they wanted. When they were all full, he said to
the disciples, "Gather the pieces left over; let us
not waste a bit." So they gathered them all and
filled twelve baskets with the pieces left over from
the five barley loaves which the people had eaten.
(John 6:1–15)

You're familiar with this story, aren't you?

It's one of the many "wow" stories in the Bible.

"Wow!" That's what those thousands who were fed
that evening exclaimed while burping contentedly after
the unexpected meal.

They realized Jesus was someone like a prophet.

He became their hero.

Well, he is my hero too.

Who else can be my hero in the Bible?

But in this story I find one of my minor heroes.

Who?

Andrew? Philip? Peter?

Uh, uh.

"There is a boy here."

(Did you miss him?)

And he also probably exclaimed, "Wow!" more than a
dozen times that evening.

Who was he?

What was his name?

Why should his name be recorded?

He was just a boy.

A boy lost in a crowd of five thousand.

"Not counting women and children," says Matthew when he tells this story himself.

For at that time, boys and women (I wonder) did not count. At least not much.

Just a boy.

A non-entity.

Come to think of it, what matters, after all, is that he was a boy.

I mean, a real boy.

And he was there, where it counted.

A boy who became an instant hero.

He saved the day that afternoon.

Did he give Jesus his bread and dried fish willingly or perhaps reluctantly?

If those were his supper, I'm sure he wasn't overenthusiastic about the idea.

There was no way he could guess what Jesus intended to do with the bread and the fish.

> Imagine . . . Just imagine . . .
> . . . that he had refused.

(Wow . . .)

That was his right and privilege.

Jesus certainly wouldn't have taken the bread and fish away from him by force, right?

That is not like Jesus.

Jesus only invited him. Only asked him for the bread and the fish.

Yes. Had the boy refused, had he kept the bread and the fish and eaten it, he would have felt his tummy happy and full that evening.

But, boy, he would have missed the chance of his life!

To become an instant celebrity.

Imagine he had said: "*Why me?* I'm sure I'm not the only guy around with bread in his shoulder bag. There are probably many other people with bread and fish. And figs. And cheese. And even wine. *Why me?*"

He could have said that.

But he didn't.

The fact is that he offered it to Jesus.

And so, that evening he had a good supper himself, indeed.

But not only himself.

Because of him—because of his generosity and unselfishness—five thousand hungry men had a full supper too.

"Not counting women and children."

(I think from now on boys ought to count.)

(And girls too.)

———

So, why you?

You're right. You're just a boy. You're just a girl.

What does Jesus need you for? How many worlds can Jesus conquer with you? With just a boy? With just a girl?

What do you have that has caught Jesus's eye?

I'm sure you can point out many of your classmates and friends who are more gifted than you.

Why, they are even more religious than you.

Then why me?

What can Jesus do with my talents? I have only a few.

That's the problem, my friend. You can never tell what Jesus can achieve with you after you've placed yourself at his disposal and service.

For Jesus, you count.

With Jesus, you count much more.

You are not much, truly.

But in the hands of Jesus . . .

So, why you?

Well, why *not* you?

———————

Now, are you sure you have nothing to tell Jesus at this point? Why don't you just close your eyes and talk to Jesus? Why don't you tell him:

"Lord, I am scared.

I hesitate to give you my bread and my fish.

Whatever I have.

I'd never know.

You might eat it yourself and leave me without supper.

For, you see, Lord, I happen to have plans of my own.

I also plan to use my talents.

I also plan to live my life.

Lord.

Are you sure your plans for me will make me happy."

Go on. Talk to Jesus.

UNUSUALLY LUCKY

God sent the angel Gabriel to a town in Galilee named Nazareth. He had a message for a girl promised in marriage to a man named Joseph, who was a descendant of King David. The girl's name was Mary. The angel came to her and said, "Peace be with you! The Lord is with you and has greatly blessed you!"

Mary was deeply troubled by the angel's message, and she wondered what his words meant. The angel said to her, "Don't be afraid, Mary; God has been gracious to you. You will become pregnant and give birth to a son, and you will name him Jesus. He will be great and will be called the Son of the Most High God. The Lord God will make him a King, as his ancestor David was, and he will be the king of the descendants of Jacob forever; his kingdom will never end!"

Mary said to the angel, "I am a virgin. How, then, can this be?"

The angel answered, "The Holy Spirit will come on you, and God's power will rest upon you. For this reason the holy child will be called the Son of God.

Remember your relative Elizabeth. It is said that she cannot have children, but she herself is now six months pregnant, even though she is very old. For there is nothing that God cannot do."

"I am the Lord's servant," said Mary; "may it happen to me as you have said." And the angel left her. (Luke 1:26–38)

This one is for you, girls.

(But also for you, boys. We're all involved in this story.)

What sort of a girl was little Miriam at five? Or at ten?

How many hours a day do you think she spent in prayer?

Is it true that the first nursery rhyme she learned was a psalm?

Is the story true which has it that she used to work some minor miracles, like instantly healing the bruised knee of a playmate?

Did she really raise to life a swallow that had drowned in the town well?

Silly questions, right?

Very silly.

She did none of these fantasies. Of this you can be sure.

She was an ordinary village girl from Nazareth, who at five played with a rag doll, and who later on helped her mother with the dishes; a girl who swept the floor in the house, learned to spin wool, knit, and bake bread and fig cakes, and also learned to press the curds into delicious cheese.

There was no doubt in anyone's mind that she was a good girl, deeply religious, more than just God-fearing. Rather, God-loving.

That was the girl.

And now, she was fifteen.

(Really? You're also fifteen?)

Well, congratulations. You're just of the same age as Mary when she got the Big News.

She was told of the Big News by the angel. He gave her the message that God wanted her to be the mother of the Messiah.

Wow!

Unexpected?

Very.

To be the mother of the Messiah was the wildest dream any girl in Israel could have at the time. But I don't think those girls were foolish enough to seriously entertain the fantasy.

Certainly not Mary. She had enough sense not to think of herself as a likely candidate.

Perhaps like you.

You never thought the Lord could have plans— great plans—for you.

And yet, there you are.

You're now wondering if God is calling you.

So, what are you going to do about it?

If ever it becomes clear to you that God is calling you, will you be ready to respond?

That was the interesting thing about Mary.

She replied in all honesty to the angel: "How can I refuse? I've never said No to the Lord. I am just his handmaid. His wish is an order for me. Let it be done as the Lord wants it.

That was it.

———————

Won't you talk to the Lord now? Would you dare tell the Lord:

"Lord,
once I find out,
I will be ready to do your will whatever it is.
I know no angel will come and tell me what you want from me.
I have only one word to say:
'Fiat.'
'Let it be done.'
And if you don't want me,
I'll also say: 'Fiat, let it be done.'
Your will, Lord,
is the only thing that matters in my life."

TAKE AIM

T hen Jesus went up a hill and called to himself the men he wanted. They came to him, and he chose twelve, whom he named apostles. "I have chosen you to be with me," he told them. "I will also send you out to preach, and you will have authority to drive out demons." (Mark 3:13–15)

It all looks so simple, right?
Well, it is.
And yet, it isn't.
Let's have this clear.
If you're toying with the idea—or if the idea is toying with you—of becoming a priest or a religious, or of entering the convent, you'd better have a clear idea of what is involved here.
It'll help you a lot.

To begin with . . .
It's Jesus who is doing the choosing, not you.
I think it's somewhere in John: "It was not you that chose me: it was I that chose you."

In other words, if you have the notion that it is you who are "toying with the idea," you who are doing the planning, you whose idea it is to become a priest or a religious, you'd better drop the thought right now.

In this business, it is Jesus who takes the initiative and no one else. He does the calling, he starts the process. Our part is only to respond, and that's it.

You have no right—no one has—to judge yourself worthy of becoming a close collaborator of Jesus. You can offer yourself anytime, and tell the Lord: "Here I am, Lord; call me if you need me." But this is not a job you apply for and for which you present your credentials and qualifications.

The Bible is clear about this. It is Jesus who does the recruiting, the inviting. It is he who calls. He goes up the hill and calls the persons he wants.

Our response might be generous, joyful, enthusiastic, wild, and all that, but it also better be grateful and humble.

And so, what's he calling for?
Basically for three things.
Let's see if we can line them up straight.

Number 1. This is how the Gospel puts it: "I have chosen you to be with me."
Clear, right?
To be a friend of Jesus.
To be one of his close disciples.
To share his life.

To work for what he works, toil for what he toils, rejoice with what makes him glad.

To love what he loves and whom he loves, and to fight what he abhors.

Let us say it.

To be his double, another Jesus.

So much for that; although, you know, there is so much to be said about it, so much more you yourself can add to it.

Number 2. "I will also send you out to preach."

The way this sounds to me, it is a share in his very mission.

To preach the Good News.

"Go and preach."

No cozy and comfortable, snug and sentimental sharing of each one's company *only*.

That is not like Jesus.

Jesus can be a friend.

Jesus *must* become our friend.

He is glad to be a friend to his own.

But he's got a job to do.

A mission given to him by his Father.

"Go and preach," that's what the Father told him.

Teach people. Enlighten their minds. Encourage them.

Tell them about God's love for them. About God's mercy and sympathy, understanding and willingness to save them and to make them his children.

To me, this is something very basic in Jesus's call.

His is a call for action.

As he was active himself

And so, in our life as disciples, there must be time for friendship, for prayer, for intimate moments of loving and sharing with him.

But there is a limit to that.

Prayer has a limit.

Sentimentality has a limit.

Romance has a limit.

And we must imitate him when he stops his prayers, his intimate conversation with his Father—when he stands up and announces: "Let's go to the other towns and preach the Good News, for that's what I was sent for."

As clear as that.

Number 3. "He gave them power to drive out demons."

In other words, he commissioned them to help people.

To help them rise above their miseries.

To drive out from them the demons of selfishness, and pettiness, and all those things that make a person "unclean," enslaved by some demons.

But also, to lead them out of the demon-like atmosphere of their lives.

Out of their squalor, their poverty, their exploitation, their ignorance, their lack of human dignity. All those things by which the poor of this world are enslaved.

And to wake up the rich and the powerful from the drunkenness of their wealth, and of their power, and of their knowledge, and of all those things that often lead them to arrogance, pride, ruthlessness, abuse, ambition, and a hardening of their hearts.

There lies the challenge for you.

For these are heavy chains with which the rich and the powerful are bound.

It's a pitiful slavery, but they love it.

A tight program. Isn't it?

A tough one, this mission of Jesus.

I'm sure you can see he will need all the help he can get.

He also sees that.

He calls people.

To be with him and work with him.

And so we respond.

Gee, I don't know whether this does anything to you.

It thrills me, I tell you.

It's something fantastic.

But tough.

And that's what makes the call so tantalizing.

Almost irresistible.

———————

Any reaction from you?

Anything you want to tell Jesus?

THE DREAMER 4

After Herod died, an angel of the Lord appeared in a dream to Joseph in Egypt and said, "Get up, take the child and his mother and go back to the land of Israel, because those who tried to kill the child are dead." So Joseph got up, took the child and his mother, and went back to Israel.

But when Joseph heard that Archelaus had succeeded his father Herod as king of Judea, he was afraid to go there. He was given more instructions in a dream, so he went to the province of Galilee and made his home in a town named Nazareth. And so what the prophets had said came true: "He will be called a Nazarene." (Matthew 2:19–23)

If you dare to go over the first two chapters of Matthew— it can be done quickly as I am sure you are familiar with the stories— you will meet an interesting character: Joseph, the Dreamer.

Have you noticed?

Angels talk to him in his dreams.

"Joseph, go and marry that girl you love, even if she is obviously pregnant."

And Joseph obliges.

"Joseph, take your family to Egypt."

And there goes Joseph, to Egypt, as his dream told him.

"Joseph, time to go back to Israel."

Back to Israel, to Bethlehem.

"No, Joseph, not Bethlehem, I meant Nazareth."

So, Nazareth it will be.

———————

I have heard many times young people say: "It's the dream of my life."

And often I smile back with pleasure.

You might be one of those people who has the ability to dream with their eyes open.

Congratulations!

Look, friend, if you do not dream while young, when will you dream?

By the way, didn't it ever occur to you that when Joseph was doing all the dreaming, he was a young man?

Oh? How young?

Maybe younger than you.

Don't forget the first dream took place when Mary and he were only sweethearts. And at that time people got married very young. Certainly before twenty. Make it seventeen or eighteen.

There is nothing wrong with dreaming.

If only one knows how to check it against reality.

To do that, Joseph, who dreamt while sleeping, only had to open his eyes and reflect.

Discern, we say now.

Come to the realization— fully awake now—that the dream meant something. That it came from God.

But in your case, because you dream mostly with your eyes open, you need to close your eyes instead.

And reflect.

Discern.

And ask yourself: Is this a dream or an illusion?

Will this lead me somewhere?

Is this dream of mine going to be backed by a life that would try to be more and more Christian?

For, you see, a vocation thrills a person, warms the heart. That is its nature. It takes a person for a flight. Up, up, all the way up.

But a vocation is also a call for action.

It pushes people to do something about it.

Beginning with themselves . . . ourselves.

If you are not growing as a Christian; if you are not getting any closer to God, you better double check your dream. You might be suffering from a delusion. You might be taken for a ride, rather than a flight.

There you are. You always wanted a hint to know if what you feel is a vocation or not.

Well, very simple. Is this idea of the vocation changing you into a better person? Is it influencing your life . . . for the better?

Yes?

Then, bingo.

Green light ahead. So far so good.

No? It's not affecting your life?

Not a good sign.

Red light?

Not sure.

But certainly yellow light. Proceed with caution. Don't take things for granted.

And keep exploring. The situation might improve.

Just close your eyes once in a while and keep asking questions.

THE LOAFER

T he next day Jesus decided to go to Galilee. He
found Philip and said to him, "Come with me!"
(Philip was from Bethsaida, the town where
Andrew and Peter lived.) Philip found Nathaniel and
told him, "We have found the one whom Moses
wrote about in the book of the Law and whom the
prophets also wrote about. He is Jesus, son of
Joseph, from Nazareth."

"Can anything good come from Nazareth?"
Nathaniel asked.

"Come and see," answered Philip.

When Jesus saw Nathaniel coming to him,
he said about him, "Here is a real Israelite; there
is nothing false in him!"

Nathaniel asked him, "How do you know me?"

Jesus answered, "I saw you when you were
under the fig tree before Philip called you."

"Teacher," answered Nathaniel, "you are the Son
of God! You are the King of Israel!"

Jesus said, "Do you believe just because I told you I saw you when you were under the fig tree? You will see much greater things than this." And he said to them, "I am telling you the truth; you will see heaven open and God's angels going up and coming down on the Son of Man." (John 1:43–51)

I don't know if good old Nathan was really loafing under the fig tree. In summer, I've seen people taking naps under the cool shade of fig trees. Certainly, at least it was under a fig tree that Jesus "saw" him. So, it's anyone's guess what Nathan was doing there.

Yet, I have the feeling that mentally, at least, he was caught napping. He was far from thinking he could be called for what he was actually called.

He did not seem to have too high an esteem of Nazareth. Nazarethans in his view were "no-gooders." And that, of course, applied to Jesus too.

On that point, Nathan was definitely loafing.

Way off target.

Here he gave proof of being a poor appraiser of men.

He did not know who Jesus really was.

He did not even know who he himself was.

A simple, but fine man.

A real Israelite. Guileless and reliable.

I imagine him walking with a peasant's ungainly, heavy gait, a well-weathered face, curious eyes, and a big, broad smile.

A good, God-fearing Israelite.

Only loafing.

He just needed to be awakened.

His horizons needed broadening beyond the parochial pettiness that led the people of Cana to look down on the Nazarethans.

I wonder what the people from Nazareth thought of the people of Cana, the Cana-ites.

Well, we know of at least one Nazarethan who thought you could find real Israelites in Cana.

The only trouble was Cana-ites seldom thought of doing anything better than rake naps under fig trees.

It has happened to many before you.

People who have golden hearts.

Fine Christians.

But who never thought they could be called.

The idea never crossed their minds that they too could be invited by Jesus to join the convent or to become a priest.

They had never been awakened by the idea.

And then, suddenly, Jesus was there.

And beckoning.

This was perhaps your case, wasn't it?

Or are you still napping?

———

All right. Why don't you talk it over with Jesus? Something like:

"Lord,

I really have no idea how good I am and at what.

But, I don't want my talents, whatever they are, to be wasted in some cheap cause.

Awaken in my heart the desire to do something great,

something that will give me a sense of fulfillment in life.

Like following you closely, for instance."

BUSINESS AS USUAL 6

J esus went back again to the shore of Lake
Galilee. A crowd came to him, and he started
teaching them. As he walked along, he saw a tax
collector, Levi, son of Alphaeus, sitting in his office.
Jesus said to him, "Follow me." Levi got up and
followed him.

Later on Jesus was having a meal in Levi's house.
A large number of tax collectors and other outcasts
was following Jesus, and many of them joined him
and his disciples at the table. Some teachers of the
Law, who were Pharisees, saw that Jesus was eating
with these outcasts and tax collectors, so they asked
his disciples, "'Why does he eat with such people?"

Jesus heard them and answered, "People who
are well do not need a doctor, but only those who
are sick. I have not come to call respectable people,
but outcasts." (Mark 2:13–17)

This Jesus is very unpredictable, right?
You never know where he will strike next.
Like a gardener walking in a garden and picking
flowers at random on his way.

Now left, now right: whichever flowers he likes.
The problem is: they aren't always the prettiest.
In fact, some of them are ugly.
The man seems to have poor taste.
Look at him: inviting a tax collector to join his team.
We are very, very surprised.
But the most surprised of all was Levi himself.
He seemed to have been so shocked that he didn't even think twice. Right then and there he told his assistant to take charge.
(Did he have an assistant?)
Or simply, he hanged on the doorknob of his office an "Out for Lunch" sign and never came back.
The "Out for Lunch" became "Out of Business."
He went into another business venture.
He found some unusual business partners.
He proved himself a shrewd businessman.
With a sharp eye for exotic business opportunities.

"Levi got up and followed him.
Just like that.
How's that for an outcast?
No dilly-dallying when he heard Jesus's call.
You'd think because he was a good tax collector, a good accountant, he would have paused for a while, and done at least some mental calculation.
His hasty decision doesn't look very much in line with his character and professional training.
But that's the way he actually did it.
I don't know what this story does to you.
It puts me to shame, if you ask me.

Some of us, before responding to Jesus's call, have kept him waiting for years.

I did.

Some of us have asked him for some time to fix things.

Time to balance our books,

Time to clear our desk.

Time to make a feasibility study.

Time to think things over.

And this could also happen to you.

Say, since when are you feeling Jesus's call?

For how long have you kept him waiting?

No. No one is recommending rash decisions. The issues must be prudently weighed.

But there is a limit to weighing, a limit to hesitation.

And there comes the moment when you have to start trusting him who is calling you.

There is time for careful calculations.

For prudent consultation.

And there is a time for generosity.

In following a vocation, the head has a role to play.

But it is not a matter of the mind.

A vocation is a matter of the heart.

Levi had done enough cold calculations in his life.

For once he followed his generous heart.

Good for him.

Good old Levi.

ARE STARS REALLY UNREACHABLE?

Jesus was born in the town of Bethlehem in Judea, during the time when Herod was King. Soon afterward, some men who studied the stars came from the East to Jerusalem and asked, "Where is the baby born to be the king of the Jews? We saw his star when it came up in the east, and we have come to worship him."

When King Herod heard about this, he was very upset, and so was everyone else in Jerusalem. He called together all the chief priests and the teachers of the Law and asked them, "Where will the Messiah be born?"

"In the town of Bethlehem in Judea," they answered. "For this is what the prophet wrote: 'Bethlehem in the land of Judah, you are by no means the least of the leading cities of Judah, for from you will come a leader who will guide my people Israel.'"

So Herod called the visitors from the East to a secret meeting and found out from them the exact time the star had appeared. Then he sent them to

Bethlehem with these instructions: "Go and make a careful search for the child; and when you find him, let me know, so that I too may go and worship him."

And so they left, and on their way they saw the same star they had seen in the East. When they saw it, how happy they were, what joy was theirs! It went ahead of them until it stopped over the place where the child was. They went into the house, and when they saw the child with his mother Mary, they knelt down and worshiped him. They brought out their gifts of gold, frankincense, and myrrh, and presented them to him.

Then they returned to their country by another road, since God had warned them in a dream not to go back to Herod. (Matthew 2:1–12)

No one really knows for sure who these gentlemen were.

Or where exactly they came from.

But two things can be safely assumed.

One: they were astrologers, stargazers. People—you could say—a little bit out of this world. More concerned with the things that hang from the skies than with the things on earth. Get the picture?

And, two: they came from afar. It took some trouble to do what they did.

Let me get down to real business.

To follow Jesus's call takes two things:
One, a clear vision to see what others do not see.
Two, lots of guts to follow what others do not follow.

———————————

The Magi weren't the only ones to see the star.
Others saw it, found it lovely and that was all.
Some understood its meaning and rejoiced in the fact that a new king had been born for the Jews.
Still some thought of going on a search for that king, but then forgot all about it.
Only the Magi put the idea into action,

Their decision drew several reactions from those who saw them making preparations for the journey.
"But are you sure?" some asked.
And the Magi didn't know what to reply, for they really weren't that sure. Not a hundred percent sure, of course.
"And do you really know what awaits you in the trip? Especially you at your age," they told the eldest of the three "Do you think you can undergo the rigors of the long journey?"
"Wish you luck," said others. And to themselves they added: "You're gonna need it."

Most people simply thought they were nuts.
Lunatics.
Moonstruck.
Too much looking at the moon and the stars had softened their brains.

Imagine! Following a star!

Hadn't they heard that stars are unreachable?

They ought to know that, oughtn't they?

It must have looked bad.

Not very encouraging, right?

They encountered misunderstanding.

A lack of support.

And yet they went ahead with their plans.

They played deaf to the cynics' sneers and unsolicited suggestions.

They just kept looking at the star that kept twinkling up there in the sky.

They kept their eyes riveted on it.

So blue, so bright, so beautiful.

So unreachable.

And yet—no doubt—beckoning.

And so, they started out after it.

And after a while they could hear no more abuse.

They witnessed no more sneers.

For they had moved away from them all.

At last.

And they were alone, all alone with their star, to which they had tied up their destinies.

I'm sure you will agree with me that they truly deserved to be rewarded.

They were courageous, so they found Jesus. They followed a star, and they found the Sun.

There were hardships along the way.

There was discouragement, loneliness, uncertainty.

It was not easy.

But an ideal animated them: they wanted to find the King.

The King was calling them.

And they had not failed him.

Look here, friend.

If you make up your mind to become a priest or enter the convent, you better be ready to overcome some obstacles.

External and internal.

Friends will misunderstand you. Or despise you.

"What a waste," your friends from the opposite sex might say.

Others will think that you are cuckoo, soft in the head. "Anyway," they will say, "he has always been a bit weird, an oddball."

And also, you'll have to put up with some inner problems.

Your determination will be put to the test.

And you will need a helper and a guide.

A priest, a confidant, someone to help you steer through all these troubles.

But, cheer up. Don't take your eyes off the star.

Keep pressing forward. One day at a time.

At the end of the journey, your reward awaits you.

Jesus.

The King.

Your Star, at last.

SEE NO EVIL

They came to Jericho, and as Jesus was leaving with his disciples and a large crowd, a blind beggar named Bartimaeus, son of Timaeus, was sitting by the road. When he heard that it was Jesus of Nazareth, he began to shout, "Jesus! Son of David! Have mercy on me!"

Many of the people scolded him and told him to be quiet. But he shouted even more loudly, "Son of David, have mercy on me!"

Jesus stopped and said, "Call him."

So they called the blind man. "Cheer up!" they said. "Get up, he is calling you."

So he threw off his cloak, jumped up, and came to Jesus.

"What do you want me to do for you?" Jesus asked him.

"Teacher," the blind man answered, "I want to see again."

"Go," Jesus told him, "your faith has made you well."

At once he was able to see and followed Jesus on the road. (Mark 10:46–52)

The vocation is an enlightenment.

It's like opening our eyes to something that has always been there, in front of our eyes, but to which our eyes were blind.

But the vocation is probably more similar to an encounter.

With a person, of course.

And you know who that person is: Jesus.

It all boils down to this: there comes a moment when Jesus suddenly means something to you. He attracts you. And inspires you.

To follow him.

Enter Barty.

Who is sitting by the road.

Does he remind you of a fence-sitter?

Sure, Barry is indifferent, blind to everything.

Blind to what is going on around him.

Blind to the fact that Jesus is passing him by.

Luckily, he was not deaf.

He could still hear.

And he heard Jesus passing by.

"Jesus, Son of David, have mercy on me.

And then the incredible happened.

"Cheer up, Barty; get up. He is calling you." And Barty opened big his cloudy eyes, frantically batted his sore

eyelids, and for the first time in his life, experienced
an intolerable thrill.

Jesus was calling him.

At once he was able to see, and he followed Jesus
on the road.

Jesus had told him to go home.

But that was out of the question.

He wanted to be a witness to him, to Jesus.

It is like that with us too.

That's the way the call often comes to us.

We sit by the road.

Indifferent.

Busy with the insignia of our mendicancy: our staff,
our coin plate, our beggar's bag and cloak.

Our status symbols.

Never ever had any wider horizon.

Until one day, in the morning, we actually hear
about Jesus.

Not that we've never heard of him before.

But this time we felt him close to us.

And then, the cheerful news, the good news:

"He is calling you."

A memorable encounter follows.

(I'm sure you've already had one with Jesus too.)

And the friendship is sealed.

We follow him.

On the road.

On the move with Jesus.

No more begging.

No more starving.
No more misery.
No more emptiness of the heart.
For Jesus has begun to fill our lives.

————————

Talk to Christ:

"Jesus,
Son of David,
have mercy on me.
No, Lord.
It's not a coin which I expect from you.
I want you to notice me sitting by the road;
I want you to call me to you,
to open my eyes,
that at last I may see you
smiling at me."

HEAR NO EVIL, SPEAK NO EVIL

Jesus then left the neighborhood of Tyre and went on through Sidon to Lake Galilee, going by way of the territory of the Ten Towns. Some people brought him a man who was deaf and could hardly speak, and they begged Jesus to place his hands on him. So Jesus took him off alone, away from the crowd, put his fingers in the man's ears, spat, and touched the man's tongue. Then Jesus looked up to heaven, gave a deep groan, and said to the man, *"Ephphatha,"* which means, "Open up!"

At once the man was able to hear, his speech impediment was removed, and he began to talk without any trouble. Then Jesus ordered the people not to speak of it to anyone; but the more he ordered them not to, the more they told it. And all who heard were completely amazed. "How well he does everything!" they exclaimed. "He even causes the deaf to hear and the dumb to speak!" (Mark 7:31–37)

I've known some young people who have felt Jesus's call.

For a while Jesus's voice was coming through loud and clear.

Then it began to grow feeble, weaker and weaker, became an almost inaudible whisper, and finally faded away for good.

In most of these cases, Jesus's call faded away because it was not properly cultivated, not properly listened to.

Those to whom it was addressed had other interests to follow, other cares to worry about.

And so their vocation died a natural death.

Look at this deaf-mute.

Jesus intended to enlighten him.

To open his ears.

To loosen the obstacle of his tongue.

First, he takes him away to a lonely place.

Where he can be alone with him.

Away from the crowd.

Where he can have his whole attention.

He is a deaf-mute.

Deaf-mutes are very sensitive people.

Filled with complexes and fears.

He'd feel ill at ease being the center of attention of a crowd.

He needs TLC.

Tender Loving Care.

Jesus has to inspire in him a sense of faith, of trust in him.

And that's just what you shouldn't try to do in the middle of a crowd.

You can't gesture to him, in front of everyone, to open his mouth big, to draw his tongue long.

The man has to be reassured first.

To be made comfortable.

Made to feel that he has nothing to fear from this stranger.

So, away, away from the crowd.

Where Jesus can smile at him reassuringly.

And make the man's confidence grow.

Where Jesus can take his time.

And use sign language.

Where Jesus can speak to him slowly and exaggerate the modulation of his words, so that the man can lip-read him.

For there are people who have gotten trapped inside their own shells.

Sensitive, shy, insecure, unaware of their potentials.

You could be one of them.

People who are closed to all—including Jesus.

Perhaps you need to be talked to kindly.

Tenderly.

Reassuringly.

For you will be drawn out of yourself only through gentle gestures.

And that can be done only in an atmosphere of intimacy.

Because of this, you've got to get away from the crowd.

Away from anything that distracts you, anything that makes it difficult for you to concentrate on Jesus.

Away from the throng, the crowd, by all means.
But also away from whatever else is crowding your life.
Effectively screening you from Jesus.
Blocking your sight of Jesus.
Making it impossible for Jesus to reach you.
People at times crowd you.
Money certainly has its bad blocking effects.
Love for comfort, worldliness, sports, idleness.
Many of these things can have a crowding effect on you.
Screening you from Jesus.

I think you'd better start a de-crowding operation.
A de-bugging operation that will unjam the reception of Jesus's voice.
For, believe it or not, the jamming takes place within you.
It is your receiver that produces those jamming effects.
Get away somewhere.
Where you can be alone with Jesus.
Make it a regular feature of your day. Spend some time in prayer with him.
Away from the crowd.
Where there is no interference.
Give Jesus a chance.
He has something to tell you.
He wants your friendship.

THIRSTY?

The Pharisees heard that Jesus was winning
and baptizing more disciples than John.
(Actually, Jesus himself did not baptize
anyone; only his disciples did.) So when Jesus heard
what was being said, he left Judea and went back
to Galilee; on his way there he had to go through
Samaria.

In Samaria he came to a town named Sychar,
which was not far from the field that Jacob had
given to his son Joseph. Jacob's well was there, and
Jesus, tired out by the trip, sat down by the well. It
was about noon.

A Samaritan woman came to draw some water,
and Jesus said to her, "Give me a drink of water." (His
disciples had gone into town to buy food.)

The woman answered, "You are a Jew, and I am
a Samaritan—so how can you ask me for a drink?"
(Jews will not use the same cups and bowls that
Samaritans use.)

Jesus answered, "If you only knew what God
gives and who it is that is asking you for a drink, you
would ask him, and he would give you life-giving
water."

"Sir," the woman said, "you don't have a bucket, and the well is deep. Where would you get that life-giving water? It was our ancestor Jacob who gave us this well; he and his sons and his flocks all drank from it. You don't claim to be greater than Jacob, do you?"

Jesus answered, "Whoever drinks this water will get thirsty again, but whoever drinks the water that I will give him will never be thirsty again. The water that I will give him will become in him a spring which will provide him with life-giving water and give him eternal life."

"Sir," the woman said, "give me that water! Then I will never be thirsty again, nor will I have to come here to draw water."

"Go and call your husband," Jesus told her, "and come back."

"I don't have a husband," she answered.

Jesus replied, "You are right when you say you don't have a husband. You have been married to five men, and the man you live with now is not really your husband. You have told me the truth."

"I see you are a prophet, sir," the woman said. "My Samaritan ancestors worshiped God on this mountain, but you Jews say that Jerusalem is the place where we should worship God."

Jesus said to her, "Believe me, woman, the time will come when people will not worship the Father either on this mountain or in Jerusalem. You Samaritans do not really know whom you worship;

but we Jews know whom we worship, because it is from the Jews that salvation comes. But the time is coming and is already here, when by the power of God's Spirit people will worship the Father as he really is, offering him the true worship that he wants. God is Spirit, and only by the power of his Spirit can people worship him as he really is."

The woman said to him, "I know that the Messiah will come, and when he comes, he will tell us everything."

Jesus answered, "I am he, I who am talking with you." (John 4:1–26)

The vocation to follow Jesus comes in several shapes, sizes, and colors.

It also comes to people in many ways.

Sometimes it comes as the natural, expected crowning of a person's lifelong friendship with Jesus.

A vocation can also be a total surprise to the person. The person may have been living his or her life, often pretty much away from God, when suddenly he or she feels God-struck.

The unthinkable suddenly becomes possible.

I wonder if this is your case.

This "experienced" girl in John's Gospel could be you. You too are aware of your "colorful" past.

And now you're puzzled. You do not know how to put these two things together: your life and your call.

This girl went on from day to day living what she thought was *her* way of life. Chasing so many fading stars. Going through so many hands. Hands that not only gave her nothing, but robbed her of the very little she had left.

And so, her life became as empty as the jar she was balancing on top of her head.

She had drunk the last drops.

There was nothing left.

Nothing to look forward to.

She had seen it all.

Tried it all.

Experienced it all.

And had found out that each new experience had left her still more drained and dry than the previous one.

No wonder she was thirsty.

And so she started off for the well.

Balancing an empty jar on her head, and in her chest a heart filled only with the hollow echoes of an unhappy, disappointing past.

And then.

Suddenly.

Bang!

It happened

How could she have known that sitting by the well and waiting for her was no other than the Messiah?

In person.

And he talked to her!

Pretended to need something from her.

This was a little ploy of his, of course. He only wanted to strike a conversation with her.

For he wanted to offer her something she needed very badly.

She could always fill her jar from old Jacob's Well.

But the heart . . . How could she fill the emptiness of her heart?

———————

Get the picture?

The past is passed.

And a vocation has nothing to do with the past.

It envisions the future.

A call doesn't have to be a reward for your past loyalty to Jesus.

Neither would your past stand in Jesus's way.

Let's put it like this:

If your past is all ruins, a heap of debris, don't worry: Jesus plans to use that too.

He will sink the foundations of a new life into it and build on top of it.

The past is buried under its own shame.

Now Jesus offers you a new life.

To make up for the emptiness of your life.

To fill the emptiness of your heart.

That thirst you feel is caused by your past.

It demands to be quenched.

It is your past that leads you to Jesus.

BE GUIDED

A man suffering from a dreaded skin disease came to Jesus, knelt down, and begged him or help. "If you want to," he said, "you can make me clean."

Jesus was filled with pity, and reached out and touched him. "I do want to," he answered. "Be clean!" At once the disease left the man, and he was clean. Then Jesus spoke sternly to him and sent him away at once, after saying to him, "Listen, don't tell anyone about this. But go straight to the priest and let him examine you; then in order to prove to everyone that you are cured, offer the sacrifice that Moses ordered."

But the man went away and began to spread the news everywhere. Indeed, he talked so much that Jesus could not go into a town publicly. Instead, he stayed out in lonely places, and people came to him from everywhere. (Mark 1:40–45)

Okay, so you don't have the man's disease. This is not your case.

But, like the man, you have also heard from Jesus the reassuring words: "Be clean."

You have also had an encounter with Jesus. And all encounters with Jesus basically follow the same pattern: they all start with an invitation from Jesus to something, which in turn calls for a response from us.

It was great.

"Be clean."

A Jesus experience.

Another "Wow!" story.

As Jesus touched his body, it underwent a marvelous transformation.

But Jesus also touched his heart.

And he was filled with joy and wonder.

Neat.

Wow!

Like in your case. Your heart was touched and your first impulse was to blabber about it to everyone.

Perhaps *blabber* is not the right word.

Let's make it *proclaim*.

Jesus frowns a bit on sudden enthusiasm.

Don't get carried away.

"Don't tell anyone about it."

If you feel Christ's call in you, treat it with respect.

There is much to be discerned about it yet.

It just might be a sudden idea that needs maturing.

People might not appreciate your ideal.

Or you might be misreading the symptoms.

And after a while, these symptoms might dissipate and simply go away.

Who knows?

And then, goodbye vocation.

People will laugh at you and make fun of you.

And rightly so. You were too quick to announce to all and sundry that you have a vocation.

Now, shame-faced, you have to admit that you never had it after all.

But one thing is always safe to do.

"Go straight to a vocation director and let yourself be guided by him or her."

Oh, yes. A vocation director is the right person to tell.

He or she should be the first person to know about it.

He or she is qualified to examine a vocation. Qualified to appraise symptoms, to interpret feelings. To see beyond the words you tell him or her and put two and two together.

Besides, he or she will keep your confidence. That's his or her job. A vocation director is a professional and will keep your search private.

Should you be afraid of consulting a vocation director?

Why should you?

Supposing, one, you do not have a vocation.

Don't fret.

The vocation director won't give you one.

No way.

He or she will only tell you that you don't have it.

Supposing, two, you read within yourself several suspicious signs, which could mean God is calling you and you *are afraid to find out*.

This could be a rather uncomfortable and unenviable position.

Because you are playing hide-and-seek with God.

Ten chances out of ten he will find you.

You can pick the choice with which you will find yourself the least uncomfortable. You can try to avoid facing God or to avoid consulting your case with a vocation director, which pretty much amounts to the same. And that is bad business.

The ostrich does that.

It buries its head in sand and pretends to see nothing.

But, my friend, you can't live all the days of your life with your head buried in sand. It soon gets hot down there. And stuffy. And sooner or later you'll have to pull your head out to breathe.

And so.

Supposing, three, you can no longer bear it and you decide to find out where you stand with God.

The vocation director is the person to go to.

He or she will sort out your tangled thoughts and feelings and strike a light in your mind.

The vocation director is very much like a jeweler, not like a doctor.

A doctor diagnoses what's wrong with a patient.

But there is nothing wrong with you.

Like a jeweler, the vocation director will take a professional look at the chunk of shiny rock you bring him or her, and he or she will tell you whether the rock is a simple colony of quartz crystals or an uncut diamond worth a fortune.

My friend, if you feel it coming and you have some doubts; if you don't know what to do, don't let that ruin the peace of your heart.

Follow Jesus' advice: "Go straight to the priest and let him examine you."

IF SYMPTOMS PERSIST, CONSULT A VOCATION DIRECTOR.

UP AND ABOUT

Jesus went back across to the other side of the lake. There at the lakeside a large crowd gathered around him. Jairus, an official of the local synagogue, arrived, and when he saw Jesus, he threw himself down at his feet and begged him earnestly, "My little daughter is very sick. Please come and place your hands on her, so that she will get well and live!"

Then Jesus started off with him. . . .

Some messengers came from Jairus house and told him, "Your daughter has died. Why bother the Teacher any longer?"

Jesus paid no attention to what they said, but told him, "Don't be afraid, only believe." Then he did not let anyone else go on with him except Peter and James and his brother John. They arrived at Jairus' house, where Jesus saw the confusion and heard all the loud crying and wailing. He went in and said to them, "Why all this confusion? Why are you crying? The child is not dead—she is only sleeping!"

They started making fun of him, so he put them all out, took the child's father and mother and his three disciples, and went into the room where the child was lying. He took her by the hand and said to her, "Talitha, koum," which means, "Little girl, I tell you to get up!"

She got up at once and started walking around. (She was twelve years old.) When this happened, they were completely amazed. But Jesus gave them strict orders not to tell anyone, and he said, "Give her something to eat." (Mark 5:21–24, 35–42)

She was just twelve.
When she had this amazing encounter with Jesus.
A man she had never known or met before.
Another one of those Jesus experiences.

"Talitha, koum."
This might sound Greek to you.
Well, it isn't. It's Aramaic, one of the languages Jesus spoke. With a Galilean accent, of course.
And it means: "Hear, little girl; stand up."

You might no longer be twelve.
And therefore be a little girl no longer.
Or you might be neither a girl nor twelve.
For you may happen to be a boy.
No matter.
You can still hear Jesus's voice: "Stand up."
Jesus's voice: "Awake from your sleep."
Jesus's voice: "What are you doing lying in bed?"

Jesus's voice: "Why so pale, so still?"
"Stand up, I tell you, stand up!"

And you did.
Unbelievable, but you did.
From where did you muster the strength?
You didn't.
When you woke up, didn't you notice that Jesus was holding you by the hand?
With his touch Jesus passed on his tremendous vitality to you, and that did it.
Jesus touched your heart.

Jesus can do that, you know?
He invites, or he commands, but he always provides his chosen ones the strength to carry out his order, or to pursue the program of life he presents.
There is nothing you ought to be afraid of. If Jesus is calling you to become a nun or a priest, he will sustain you along the way.
He will hold you by the hand.
This is especially true in the beginning.
When the going is more difficult.
Afterwards, when you're up and about, he expects you to get stronger until you can be on your own.
Actually we're never quite on our own. For Jesus is always standing by us.
But he wants you to learn how to take care of yourself.
A vocation has to be fostered, and nurtured and watered; and fertilizer has to be applied to it.

"Give her something to eat."

Get it?

Your vocation needs prayer to grow. Daily prayer.

Serene, serious, sincere reflection.

You need to read about Jesus, to read his Gospel daily.

Like this girl, who needed food to keep herself in good health afterwards.

Jesus will not be making everyday miracles for you.

You cannot let your vocation wither and die.

A pity, indeed.

If after a fine start, it would came to naught.

For lack of follow-up.

———————

"Lord,

I hear you all right.

Your voice, firm and in command, reaches the inner ear of my heart, telling me to stand up and start moving.

Lend me your hand, Lord.

That leaning on it,

I may take the first faltering steps out of my slumber.

And whenever I am about to give up or feel so weak that I am about to collapse onto a heap, hold me up, Lord, and order me again:

"Stand up and move;

take and eat, and get strong again."

DEEP FREEZE

A man named Lazarus, who lived in Bethany, became sick. Bethany was the town where Mary and her sister Martha lived. (This Mary was the one who poured the perfume on the Lord's feet and wiped them with her hair; it was her brother Lazarus who was sick.) The sisters sent Jesus a message: "Lord, your dear friend is sick."

When Jesus heard it, he said, "The final result of this sickness will not be the death of Lazarus; this has happened in order to bring glory to God, and it will be the means by which the Son of God will receive glory."

Jesus loved Martha and her sister and Lazarus. Yet when he received the news that Lazarus was sick, he stayed where he was for two more days. Then he said to the disciples, "Let us go back to Judea."

"Teacher," the disciples answered, just a short time ago the people there wanted to stone you; and are you planning to go back?"

Jesus said, "A day has twelve hours, doesn't it? So whoever walks in broad daylight does not stumble, for he sees the light of this world. But if he walks during the night he stumbles, because he has no light." Jesus said this and then added, "Our friend Lazarus has fallen asleep, but I will go and wake him up."

The disciples answered, "If he is asleep, Lord, he will get well."

Jesus meant that Lazarus had died, but they thought he meant natural sleep. So Jesus told them plainly, "Lazarus is dead, but for your sake I am glad that I was not with him, so that you will believe. Let us go to him."

Thomas (called the Twin) said to his fellow disciples, "Let us all go along with the Teacher, so that we may die with him!"

When Jesus arrived, he found that Lazarus had been buried four days before. Bethany was less than two miles from Jerusalem, and many Judeans had come to see Martha and Mary to comfort them about their brother's death.

When Martha heard that Jesus was coming, she went out to meet him, but Mary stayed in the house. Martha said to Jesus, "If you had been here, Lord, my brother would not have died! But I know that even now God will give you whatever you ask him for."

"Your brother will rise to life," Jesus told her.

I know," she replied, "that he will rise to life on the last day."

Jesus said to her, "I am the resurrection and the life. Whoever believes in me will live, even though he dies; and whoever lives and believes in me will never die. Do you believe this?"

"Yes, Lord!" she answered. "I do believe that you are the Messiah, the Son of God, who was to come into the world."

After Martha said this, she went back and called her sister Mary privately. "The Teacher is here," she told her, "and is asking for you." When Mary heard this, she got up and hurried out to meet him. (Jesus had not yet arrived in the village, but was still in the place where Martha had met him.) The people who were in the house with Mary comforting her followed her when they saw her get up and hurry out. They thought that she was going to the grave to weep there.

Mary arrived where Jesus was, and as soon as she saw him, she fell at his feet. "Lord," she said, "if you had been here, my brother would not have died!"

Jesus saw her weeping, and he saw how the people with her were weeping also; his heart was touched, and he was deeply moved. "Where have you buried him?" he asked them.

"Come and see, Lord," they answered.

Jesus wept.

"See how much he loved him!" the people said. But some of them said, "He gave sight to the blind man, didn't he? Could he not have kept Lazarus from dying?"

Deeply moved once more, Jesus went to the tomb, which was a cave with a stone placed at the entrance. "Take the stone away," Jesus ordered.

Martha, the dead man's sister, answered, "There will be a bad smell, Lord. He has been buried four days!"

Jesus said to her, "Didn't I tell you that you would see God's glory if you believed?" They took the stone away. Jesus looked up and said, "I thank you, Father, that you listen to me. I know that you always listen to me, but I say this for the sake of the people here, so that they will believe that you sent me." After he had said this, he called out in a loud voice, "Lazarus, come out!" He came out, his hands and feet wrapped in grave cloths, and with a cloth around his face. "Untie him," Jesus told them, "and let him go." (John 11:1–44)

Lazarus, Jesus's friend.

While at Jerusalem, Jesus would always lodge at nearby Bethany, at the place of his friend Lazarus.

Only with Lazarus did he feel at home.

And safe.

For by then Jerusalem was no longer safe for Jesus.

("Lord,
 do you feel safe in my heart?
 Is my heart the heart of a friend?
 My heart is always open for you to lodge
in any time.

Come in, Lord, feel at home.
Make yourself comfortable.")

And then, the bad and unexpected news: "Your best friend Lazarus is very sick."

Jesus would never abandon a friend.

Unless . . .

Unless it is too late.

For by the time word reached Jesus, his friend was already dead and about to be buried.

But Jesus insisted he was only asleep.

Exactly what he said about the twelve-year-old girl, Jairus's daughter.

It was the sleep of death, sure.

But to Jesus he was only asleep.

And he would not let his friend sleep forever.

He would call his friend Lazarus out of his miserable condition.

———

"Lazarus, come out!"

The stone had been rolled. The only thing that blocked communication between Jesus and Lazarus.

"Lazarus, come our!"

Jesus was now stooping towards the chamber-tomb. He couldn't help capping his nose with his hand.

Sleeping people do not smell, corpses do.

"Lazarus, come out!"

He had to shout. He had to use his powerful and beautiful voice at full blast. Just like when be calmed the storm in the lake.

Only Jesus's powerful voice can pierce ears rendered deaf by death.

Lazarus came to from his deep-freeze and woke up.

Jesus's voice was calling him.

Friendship was summoning.

You too can lapse into a deep-freeze.

Through sheer stolidity of course.

Only the dumbest sort of negligence can lead to it.

A wound in the soul that is allowed to fester, a sickness that goes on unattended, can lead to a situation of sleep-death.

The stench of decay spreads fast about that person.

Spiritually he has become a corpse.

And Jesus senses it.

Only Jesus can bring him back to life.

Only Jesus does not abandon a friend even if he stinks.

It will take some powerful shouting. It will cost him some groaning and shedding of tears.

But Jesus won't give on you up, even if you start to discharge a stink.

You see, hope is never lost when you have a friend as powerful and as loyal as Jesus.

If ever you reach this state of non-life, and you hear Jesus's voice again, you must wake up.

And believe the unbelievable.

That you are alive again.

That the stone has been rolled and light is coming again into the dimness of your gloomy world.

When again the voice of Jesus stirs up your consciousness, do what Lazarus did:

Stretch your stiff muscles.

Flex your rigid limbs.

Peel off your bandages and shed off your funereal linen, all that stuff around you that has been stifling life in you.

Then blink as fast as you can and get used to the light for you are crawling out into the world of sunshine again.

Where Jesus waits for you.

To give you a big hear hug.

Back to life.

Back to light.

Back to friendship.

Back to where you were before. Not all has been lost.

It's time to celebrate. For you were asleep and woke up.

Once more, Jesus has saved you.

"Lord, Lord.

It frightens me to think that one day I could leave your friendship and fall out of the world of the living.

Let this never happen to me, Lord.

Please, never allow my problems to fester in my heart to the point of endangering my life with you.

And if this ever happens, let the memory of our friendship move you to compassion and tears over me.

And bring me back from my death.

And I promise, Lord, that if I ever die,

I'll keep an ear still tuned to your voice,

so that it may be stirred back to life by your voice again."

A SURPRISE ATTACK

In the meantime Saul kept up his violent threats of murder against the followers of the Lord. He went to the High Priest and asked for letters of introduction to the synagogues in Damascus, so that if he should find there any followers of the Way of the Lord, he would be able to arrest them, both men and women, and bring them back to Jerusalem.

As Saul was coming near the city of Damascus, suddenly a light from the sky flashed around him. He fell to the ground and heard a voice saying to him, "Saul, Saul! Why do you persecute me?"

"Who are you, Lord?" he asked.

"I am Jesus, whom you persecute," the voice said. "But get up and go into the city, where you will be told what you must do."

The men who were traveling with Saul had stopped, not saying a word; they heard the voice but could not see anyone. Saul got up from the ground and opened his eyes, but could not see a thing. So they took him by the hand and led him into Damascus. For three days he was not able to see, and during that time he did not eat or drink anything.

There was a Christian in Damascus named Ananias. He had a vision, in which the Lord said to him, "Ananias!"

"Here I am, Lord," he answered.

The Lord said to him, "Get ready and go to Straight Street, and at the house of Judas ask for a man from Tarsus named Saul. He is praying, and in a vision he has seen a man named Ananias come in and place his hands on him so that he might see again."

Ananias answered, "Lord many people have told me about this man and about all the terrible things he has done to your people in Jerusalem. And he has come to Damascus with authority from the chief priests to arrest all who worship you."

The Lord said to him, "Go, because I have chosen him to serve me, to make my name known to Gentiles and kings and to the people of Israel. And I myself will show him all that he must suffer for my sake."

So Ananias went, entered the house where Saul was, and placed his hands on him. "Brother Saul," he said, "the Lord has sent me—Jesus himself, who appeared to you on the road as you were coming here. He sent me so that you might see again and be filled with the Holy Spirit." At once something like fish scales fell from Saul's eyes, and he was able to see again. He stood up and was baptized; and after he had eaten, his strength came back. (Acts 9:1–19)

Saul was far from ready for his Damascus experience.

He was the Christians' public enemy number one.

He persecuted them.

He hated Jesus.

It looked bad for the group of believers.

He was bent on destroying the movement in the bud.

He knew the believers' identities, their leaders, and meeting places.

But there was something he did not know.

That he was a marked man.

Precisely by the founder of the Christians, by Jesus.

Jesus had written the name "Saul of Tarsus" in his pocket notebook, we could say.

Jesus often acts in mysterious ways.

He tags people secretly and leads them through twists and turns to where he wants.

What good did Jesus see in Saul?

My guess is this: At the bottom of his heart, Saul was an honest man.

He was honestly convinced that Christians were wrong and wayward.

And he felt it his duty to religion and to God to defend what he thought was the truth.

The Jewish truth.

Saul, the most zealous persecutor of the early Church.

What can you do to achieve the impossible task of turning him around and transforming him into its most tenacious apostle?

If Saul was an honest man, the task was simple, if a little strong.

Dazzle him with light.

There's something an honest person will never bring himself to do: to fight light. To fight truth.

"Saul, Saul! Why do you persecute me?"

Saul's answer tells us the method was working.

Interesting what he replied:

"Who are you, Lord?" Did you notice it?

"Lord."

He blurted it out.

He called his worst enemy "Lord."

At that moment, Saul had already surrendered to Jesus.

Down on the ground as he was, and blinded by light, he knew he had been conquered.

In a fair contest.

Jesus immediately went into action.

There was no time to waste.

There were countless churches to be founded.

Communities to be established all over the world.

"Get up, Saul. Orders are waiting for you in the city."

End of the struggle.

It is time to rebuild.

And the Lord happens to be in a hurry.

I am tempted to give you some advice.

Don't you ever try to fight Jesus if you know what's good for you.

Sometimes I argue with him.

Useless!

Ten times out of ten, I lose.

No.

Don't misunderstand me.

It's okay to have a friendly argument with Jesus.

It's a sign that you feel comfortable with him.

Some saints used to bargain with him.

The great Sr. Teresa of Avila did a few times.

You can try it. Just be ready to lose, okay?

And one more thing.

Never run away from the light.

Know what I mean?

It takes courage to stare at the light.

It is cowardice to shut your eyes tight against what you see clearly.

Not Saul. He wouldn't do that.

For Saul was an honest man.

At Damascus, he bravely faced a new life.

The unknown.

He was following a call.

Or rather obeying a dispatch of fresh orders. But something had seized him. And that something was giving him an odd feeling of confidence.

He who had given him the order to go into the city identified himself with these words: "I am Jesus."

Jesus, his conqueror.

Jesus, his former enemy.

Jesus, his Lord.

It was a strange feeling. Very strange it was.

But it was a beautiful feeling. Very beautiful it was.

Wow!

————————

"Lord,

it feels great to know you might have marked me before I even suspected it.

You have assigned to me a mission to fulfill in life.

I need your light right now,

to know what you want from me.

Or what you want for me.

Don't dazzle me, Lord. I am a friend.

Just tell me who you are.

Let me know you are behind these feelings I sense inside.

UP A TREE

Jesus went on into Jericho and was passing through. There was a chief tax collector there named Zacchaeus, who was rich. He was trying to see who Jesus was, but he was a little man and could not see Jesus because of the crowd. So he ran ahead of the crowd and climbed a sycamore tree to see Jesus, who was going to pass that way. When Jesus came to that place, he looked up and said to Zacchaeus. "Hurry down, Zacchaeus, because I must stay in your house today."

Zacchaeus hurried down and welcomed him with great joy. All the people who saw it started grumbling, "This man has gone as a guest to the home of a sinner!"

Zacchaeus stood up and said to the Lord, "Listen, sir! I will give half my belongings to the poor, and if have cheated anyone, I will pay him back four times as much."

Jesus said to him. "Salvation has come to this house today, for this man, also, is a descendant of Abraham. The son of Man came to seek and to save the lost." (Luke 19:1–10)

At times it isn't easy to see Jesus.

Or to know what he wants from us.

But if we keep searching, we will eventually find out.

Remember that thing about "Seek and you will find?"

Neat.

But sometimes you keep on seeking only to find yourself in an even bigger confusion.

Well, perhaps you can learn from Zacchaeus.

He was a short fellow.

The only one about whom the Bible says was "short of stature."

But short stature is no hindrance in seeing Jesus.

Even if there is a human barricade towering in front of you.

In your desire to see Jesus and follow his call you too could encounter a tall human wall that may prevent you from doing so.

For instance, your parents . . .

And the plans they have for you.

For instance, a special person . . .

That boyfriend or girlfriend of yours.

No matter how tall you try to stand on the balls of your feet, you are no match for the wall. The wall is all you can see in front of your eyes.

A forbidding wall.

Or a charming wall.

A wall nonetheless.
Effectively blocking your view of Jesus.

A wall you will have to do something about.
Climb it.
Go around it.
Ignore it.
Or get yourself to a vantage point.
Follow your star.

Focus on Jesus who happens to be passing by.
For all you know he might be looking out for you too (but can't see you either).

Zacchaeus was short. So he looked for a perch—a sycamore tree from which he could get a glimpse of Jesus.
He finally saw.
And was seen.
And was called.

Come down, Zecchaeus: drop from your perch this side of the human wall that stands between you and me.
Make room for me at your table today, Zacchaeus, I want to be your guest.
Do not open those surprised eyes so wide, Zacchaeus, for I am well known to eat and drink and lodge with sinners like you.
Make room in your little life for me, Zacchaeus.

Zacchaeus couldn't believe his ears. He thought he was dreaming.

But when he saw through the leaves of the sycamore tree the faces of all his town mates turned up towards him, then he understood that, indeed, he was not dreaming.

So he climbed down.

(Or did he just drop like a ripe fruit?)

It is written he did it in a hurry.
And with joy.
Zacchaeus finally received Jesus in his home.
And in his life.

It takes joy to follow Jesus.
But it also takes generosity.
Joy + Generosity = Enthusiasm.
Enthusiasm = Wow!

Enthusiasm to overcome walls.
Made of the things of this world.
Persons.
Money.
Sins and sinful attitudes and habits.
Persons have to be left aside.
Money and possessions have to be given to the poor.
Sins have to be atoned for.
Lifestyle has to change.
Like at the big sales, EVERYTHING MUST GO.

I like what the Great Teresa of Ávila wrote:

> "Let nothing disturb you
> let nothing frighten you
> all things will come to an end
> God never changes
> patience obtains everything
> he who has God lacks nothing
> God alone is enough."

If you want to follow Jesus in the religious or priestly life, you'd better be ready to make this short verse your rule of life.

I have this poem on my desk, under the glass top.

It tantalizes me.
And haunts me. It disturbs my peace.
But, it also makes me pray: "My God and my all."

––––––––

Now, how about the original Spanish text of Teresa?

> "Nada·te turbe
> nada te espante
> todo se pasa
> dios no se muda
> la paciencia
> todo lo alcanza
> quien a dios tiene
> nada le falta
> solo dios basta."
>
> Teresa de Jesús

GIVE AND TAKE

As Jesus and his disciples went on their way, he came to a village where a woman named Martha welcomed him in her home. She had a sister named Mary, who sat down at the feet of the Lord and listened to his teaching. Martha was upset over all the work she had to do, so she came and said, "Lord, don't you care that my sister has left me to do all the work by myself? Tell her to come and help me!"

The Lord answered her, "Martha, Martha! You are worried and troubled over so many things, but just one is needed. Mary has chosen the right thing, and it will not be taken away from her." (Luke 10:38–42)

Two women.
Two sisters.
Two styles.
Two ways of receiving Jesus in their home, of accepting Jesus in their lives.
Two ways of following Jesus, then?
Two kinds of vocation? Two paths to Jesus?

Martha is all action, three times action.

Efficiency. Business.

Everything must be well-oiled and organized.

She is also plenty of noise. With the pots and the pans and the plates. And the chairs and tables.

Martha knows by experience that action makes lots of noise.

She is not sure noise does any good.

But she goes on making noise. At least it gives the impression that something is going on.

Some people think they have been called to move endlessly and make noise.

They say it's their charisma, their particular call.

In noise they somehow find self-fulfillment.

Hopefully it is not also some form of self-deception.

Always moving from one place to another.

Now the kitchen, then the dining room, then the pantry, only to scurry back to the kitchen in the end.

Always on the move.

Nervously, of course.

They thrive on restlessness.

It fine-tunes them into high gear.

Vrooom, vroom . . . they zoom off early in the morning, screeching tires and waking up the neighborhood.

It's the action principle converted into noise principle.

They can't stand stillness.

And they can't stand those who love stillness.

Martha can seldom stand having Mary around.

It's not that Mary makes Martha feel guilty.

It's just that Martha finds Mary too selfish in her complacency.

Perhaps she finds her too self-possessed. At peace with herself.

And that hurts Martha.

When there's so much to do around, how can Mary spend so much time passively listening to Jesus?

Spend perhaps is not the word that comes to her mind.

Secretly Martha thinks the proper word is *waste*.

But she won't dare say it aloud because the Master himself seems to be on the side of her sister. And Martha doesn't want to offend the Master.

For she also loves him. Honest.

After all, it's him that she frets about.

Yet the Lord doesn't seem to notice her at all.

He keeps his peace, placidly chatting about God's Kingdom with Mary and some friends around him.

"Lord, why don't you tell my sister to help me?"

Nagging Martha.

Bellyaching Martha!

(Insecurity?)

In reality she might be frantic about her identity, her mission in life.

In the meanwhile, Mary looks at the Master and smiles, delighted with his reply to Martha.

And Mary lets her be.

This is precisely what gets Martha.
That Mary lets her and everything else just be.
Doing nothing about it.
Indifferent to all.

Marys are galore in the world.
Their vocation seems to be to spend their lives
in gratifying conversation with Jesus.
Away from the world and its problems.
Anyway, those are the world's problems, not their
problems.
Is it because of indifference? Escapism?
If this is the case, then Martha might have a point
there.
For the world never rests.
And neither does God.
(Except on Sundays! Or is it the Sabbath?)

———————

Even in religious and priestly life, there are many
paths to follow.
Different ways to reach the Lord.
They're all narrow! That's a common characteristic.
Some paths cross pleasant meadows filled with
wild lilies, with a velvety view of swaying silken grass.
Etcetera, etcetera.
Their course is restful and soothing.
It is the path for the poets of God.

Others prefer more adventurous paths. Trails hacked out through ranges and ravines, timberlands and thickets.

Etcetera, etcetera.

They find the meadows too bland for their taste.

These are the divine "managers," the eternally restless of God.

No matter what path you take, you'd better make yourself ready for a fair share of lilies and thistles, of rain and sunshine, of rest and labor.

Jesus's saying that "These things must be done without neglecting the others" applies here too.

A life exclusively dedicated to prayer looks suspicious.

It appears un-Christlike.

At least that's not how Jesus saved the world.

On the other hand, action without prayer is empty.

Gong-beating.

Shadow boxing.

The formula must exclude none. It must strike a balance between both action and prayer.

Prayer alone is not enough to save the world.

Action alone is not enough to save the world.

Any life that accepts only one of these elements will not look like Christ's life.

Make sure the particular form of religious or priestly life you choose is a life where there is not only concern for this decaying world, but also some form of active commitment to redeem it.

In each religious family, the recipe might be a bit heavier on one or the other. It doesn't have to be an exact 50/50 arrangement. A mixture of a different proportion will make the cake of religious or priestly life spicier or sweeter, lighter or heavier, sharper or blander, to suit your taste and personality.

Make sure to find in your active life some time you can afford to waste every day with God.

And make sure to have in the midst of your contemplation of God some time to spend in directly helping those who still haven't heard of the Good News.

> Because of only one reason.
> The Lord did both.
> He prayed daily. (Or nightly.)
> He led an amazingly active life.
> He found time for both.
> That is the secret of an apostolic vocation.

THREE'S COMPANY

After John had been put in prison, Jesus went to Galilee and preached the Good News from God. "The right time has come," he said, "and the Kingdom of God is near! Turn away from your sins and believe the Good News!"

As Jesus walked along the shore of Lake Galilee, he saw two fishermen, Simon and his brother Andrew, catching fish with a net. Jesus said to them, "Come with me, and I will teach you to catch men." At once they left their nets and went with him.

He went a little farther on and saw two other brothers, James and John, the sons of Zebedee. They were in their boat getting their nets ready. As soon as Jesus saw them, he called them; they left their father Zebedee in the boat with the hired men and went with Jesus. (Mark 1:14–20)

Jesus has no use for loners.
He is no Lone Ranger himself.
He works with a team.

His followers make a flock, and live as a flock, and are saved within and as a flock.

Mavericks do not fit into Jesus's design to save the world.

So, his collaborators work in a team.

And the stars, the prima donnas are out of it.

No star shines when the Sun is around.

So Jesus, right from the very beginning, gathered a group to work with him.

And to share his life.

Day and night.

Come, Simon.

Come, Andrew.

You too, James and John, come and join me.

The first Christian community.

The first four around the person of Jesus.

In the following weeks, it would grow in numbers.

Up to twelve.

Very much around Jesus.

They left their families, their boats, their nets, and cast in their lot with Jesus.

To form Jesus's family.

If you want to be a star, go and join a circus.

Do your solo balancing act on the tight rope.

If you want to be the one whom all the spotlights gawk upon, do not get yourself into the religious or priestly life.

For there, the only Superstar on center stage is Jesus. And he needs no spotlight. He is light himself.

Religious life is a life of evangelical poverty. Trying to mirror the simplicity of life of those who made up the Jesus company.

This is the degree of poverty you reach after you leave everything you once held dear.

Your only possession will be Jesus, and the company of the brothers or sisters.

This is only too true in religious life.

It is a community life built around Jesus.

Forming a family.

With gives and takes.

Where there are moments of peace and joy, and moments of little tensions and conflicts like in any healthy family.

It is a life of mutual acceptance.

Achieved not without a certain amount of pain and sacrifice.

Where some members are more generous than others. Or better mixers than others. Or better workers than others.

And some holier than others.

It is the presence of Jesus in their midst that makes all the difference.

For after all, everyone in the community is animated by the same idea—to follow Jesus closely.

To work with him for the Kingdom.

No other worries in life.

No personal ambitions save that of being outstanding in the service of Jesus.

No family of their own to worry about.
No business empire to build.
No capital to leave to their posterity
The Kingdom is all they want and pursue.
The Kingdom is all-pervading.
All-encompassing.

And one more thing: it is forever.
The commitment should be final.
The break with the "world" irreparable.
All final and total.
Jesus will not accept anything less than that.
Only then can a person truly exclaim: "My God and my all."

THE
GOODY-GOODY TOO

The next day John was standing there again with two of his disciples, when he saw Jesus walking by. "There is the Lamb of God!" he said.

The two disciples heard him say this and went with Jesus. Jesus turned, saw them following him, and asked. "What are you looking for?"

They answered, "Where do you live, Rabbi?" (This word means "Teacher.")

"Come and see," he answered. (It was then about four o'clock in the afternoon.) So they went with him and saw where he lived, and spent the rest of that day with him.

One of them was Andrew, Simon Peter's brother. At once he found his brother Simon and told him. "We have found the Messiah." (This word means "Christ.") Then he took Simon to Jesus.

Jesus looked at him and said, "Your name is Simon son of John, but you will be called Cephas." (This is the same as Peter and means "a rock.") (John 1:35–42)

This wasn't the call yet. Only the acquaintance.
But that's how it all started.

They were good people.
Jesus could have said about all of them what he said about Nathaniel: "Here are some no-nonsense Israelites, nothing plastic about them."
It's good to know Jesus also called good people.
Lest we get the wrong impression that Jesus only eyes sinners and misfits to form his team.
Andrew and John, Peter, Philip, James, Nathaniel were all Israelites in good standing, who were awaiting the arrival of the Messiah.
They were simple people who, once they discovered him, did not hesitate to join him.

When he called them, they weren't shocked.
Never did they assume anything.
But neither were they surprised.
Their response leapt naturally from their lips: "Sure, Master, why not?"

Discipleship was not an alien notion to them.
Most of them, if not all, were already disciples.
Not of Jesus.
Of John.
It was the next best thing.
Before Jesus made his appearance, John was the person who came closest to their idea of a "Master."
Around John this bunch of idealists had gathered. With him they shared common ideals and lifestyle.

Which included perhaps surviving on locusts and wild honey.

And probably allowing their hair and fingernails grow freely, untouched —"undefiled" would better reflect what they thought of it all, by scissors or other metal.

It was a long and venerable tradition in Israel.

And of course, wine was a no-no with John and his disciples.

They were people filled with good will.

They did what they were taught.

Until they came in touch with Jesus.

And then they knew better.

The Kingdom had arrived.

And Jesus was calling. They were the first and the best.

It is but natural for Jesus to call to the priestly and religious life the best among the best of his Christians.

Authentic, no-nonsense Christians, nothing plastic about them.

He offers them a challenge.

It is a fact that the best priests and religious often come from families that are deeply Christian.

Boys and girls who have lived the Christian spirit since their childhood.

A Christian family is the best nursery for priestly and religious vocations.

And this may probably be your case.

Do not be surprised.

You may have been marked even before you were born.

Jesus wanted you even then.

And he has guided you through childhood to prepare you for this.

Your vocation is meant to be the crowning of a healthy Christian life in a Christian family.

By the way, you never thought your vocation has been gifted you, courtesy of your parents?

They have acted as agents for Jesus.

Now it is your turn to respond.

The challenge is right in front of you, staring at you.

And the challenge has a name: Jesus.

Jesus can use "authentic Israelites," like you.

Will you let him? ??

THE NAME
OF THE GAME
PART ONE

The Kingdom of heaven is like this. A man happens to find a treasure hidden in a field. He covers it up again, and is so happy that he goes and sells everything he has, and then goes back and buys that field.

"Also, the Kingdom of heaven is like this. A man is looking for fine pearls and when he finds one that is unusually fine, he goes and sells everything he has, and buys that pearl. (Matthew 13:44–46)

I think these two parables are two jewels themselves.

They are key parables too. For they describe the Kingdom of Heaven.

Your vocation is like a treasure hidden in the field of your heart.

A pearl of great value.

It would be wrong, however, to think you're God's only darling or something just because you have a vocation.

The vocation to the religious or priestly life is not basically different from the vocation for Christian life.

It is the same.

Plus something added to it: service.

And something demanded from it: total commitment to the Kingdom.

Let me try to glean a few traits of your vocation from these parables.

One. These two men happen to stumble upon a treasure or a pearl.

To stress the point that no one deserves to be called.

The vocation is a gift, unexpected, undeserved.

It is a privilege offered to some, not to all.

Two. The first man "in his joy" buries the treasure again and buys the field.

This joy is a key factor to determine if one's vocation is genuine or not.

If the thought of the vocation doesn't stir some kind of joy in your heart, your vocation is doubtful. It just doesn't ring right.

If you don't feel happiness in getting rid of your worldly possessions; if you do not do it with alacrity like the four fishermen did, like Zacchaeus and Levi did, then you and I are not talking about the same thing.

The option for the Kingdom of God always gives an unusual joy and a deep peace in the heart.

Jesus accepts none into his service but the joyous volunteers.

No sad-faces are accepted into Jesus's team.

Three. Both men sold everything they had and bought the field and the pearl.

That is the secret of their joy.

No sacrifice seems too stiff to win the treasure, the pearl.

They both sell and pawn anything of value they can lay their hands on.

They will not let their good fortunes pass them by.

It's the chance of their lives.

The awaited break to make it big.

All—*absolutely all*—for the Kingdom.

This is the name of the game.

Part one.

The vocation is a treasure.

The vocation is a pearl.

For to join Jesus, and work with him for the Kingdom should mean much more to you than anything else in life.

And because of this, you should be willing to abandon the persons and the things most dear to you: your parents, the hope of building your own family, your ambition in life, comfort and leisure: all must be sacrificed for the Kingdom.

It is for this reason that priestly, and especially religious life, is said to be a life of witness to the values of the Gospel.

What the Gospel stands for.

If you finally decide to join the priesthood or allow God to lead you to the religious life, you will proclaim to all and sundry that to follow the Gospel is for you the most and the only important thing in this world.

It takes an expert in pearls to appreciate an unusually rare piece. Not all can tell the difference.

But the priest or the religious does.

And he or she smiles, thinking with St. Paul: "I know to whom I have entrusted myself."

THE NAME
OF THE GAME
PART TWO

You are the salt of all mankind. But if salt loses its saltiness, there is no way to make it salty again. It has become worthless, so it is thrown out and people trample on it.

You are like light for the whole world. A city built on a hill cannot be hid. No one lights a lamp and puts it under a bowl; instead he puts it on the lamp stand, where it gives light for everyone in the house. In the same way your light must shine before people, so that they will see the good things you do and praise your Father in heaven. (Matthew 5:13–16)

Needless to say, these words of Jesus apply to all Christians.

By all means.

Holiness is not the monopoly of priestly or religious life.

To be light, to be salt is the call, the privilege and duty of every Christian.

But it must be said that those words more intensely and particularly apply to priests and religious.

For the reason that they are called to live the Gospel more intensely and more genuinely than "common mortals."

The fact is that the Christian people look upon the priests not as public servants or Church government employees, but as pastors and guides.

And so the Church's regular troops have the right to expect from them not only guidance, but also inspiration and encouragement.

As for religious, they follow a special path, corresponding to a special grace or "qualification."

That grace is technically called *charisma*, a gift received from God.

Maybe you too have received this charisma, this gift.

If you decide to respond to it, and become a religious or a priest, then you ought to know what sort of business you're getting yourself into.

You're being set on the lamp stand.

You become the city on top of the hill.

While the valley below is still enveloped in the morning mist, the whitened walls of the city on top of the hill are already glistening with the reflected rays of the rising sun.

It's goodbye to anonymity.

Simply put, the priest or religious has no right to mediocrity.

He or she must be minimally outstanding, to say the least, in giving life witness to the Gospel.

That's what's expected from the religious. That's the burden he or she assumes.

As a class, priests and religious are fulfilling that function quite well in the Church, by and large.

And this is why individual failures are more noticeable.

A regular Christian who does not faithfully live the Gospel is hardly ever noticed.

A priest or religious who adopts worldly values and manners scandalizes the people of God.

So, let not that "lamp stand" thing dazzle you.

If you daydream of being the center of attention up there at the altar, or at the pulpit, you might as well forget the whole idea.

If you love being on the candlestick so that all eyes will be fascinated by the flicker of your light, give the illusion up before it's too late.

For the call is not a call to glamour.

It is a call to service.

And so, to sober the minds of the volatile, Jesus first calls us the salt of the earth.

I'd prefer you stick to this metaphor.

You won't go wrong if you see your vocation as a vocation to be salt in the Church.

There is no glamour in being simple salt crystals.

No magic.

No glitter.

Its quiet, hidden job is seasoning people's lives while dissolving in the process.

Self-dissolution, the spending of self, the dying of self for the sake of others.

It frightens me at times.

It frightened Jesus too.

And yet he chose to become the grain of wheat who accepted death in order to bloom and bear fruit in the form of an ear of corn with many grains.

Yielding a hundredfold.

This and no other is the vocation of the priest or the religious.

You also want to be the light of the world?

Fine.

Be on top of the candlestick, all right.

But be a candle.

Burn yourself out while lighting the path of those who otherwise would walk in darkness.

Beautiful, right?

To be consumed in the service of others.

To encourage and support the Christian community by offering an outstanding example, not of power, wisdom, management abilities or oratorical gifts.

But of humility, self-sacrifice, self-spending in the service of Christ's people.

Get the point?

THE NAME OF THE GAME

PART THREE

The eleven disciples went to the hill in Galilee where Jesus had told them to go. When they saw him, they worshiped him, even though some of them doubted. Jesus drew near and said to them, "I have been given all authority in heaven and on earth. Go, then, to all peoples everywhere and make them my disciples: baptize them in the name of the Father, the Son, and the Holy Spirit, and teach them to obey everything I have commanded you. And I will be with you always, to the end of the age." (Matthew 28:16–20)

You've just read the very end of the Gospel by Matthew.

Jesus's last words on earth.

The final punch line.

Go out and preach the Good News.

That's what I chose you for.

Go out and make disciples.

Leave no corner undusted, no stone unturned.

Go to the whole world.

Go. Get on the move.

I am sending you. In the name of him who sent me.

And so, the missionary Church was born.

An ever-expanding Church.

The Church did not simply start. She exploded.

And her first big bang came with these words of Jesus.

A process of expansion was started. A process that is still going on.

Ever expanding, pushing her borders ever farther.

These last words of Jesus on earth became a force that is still impelling the Church to preach the Gospel.

The Church is either missionary or is no Church at all.

The Christian is an apostle or is no Christian at all.

Christianity is a communicable "disease." And we Christians are all "carriers."

And so, Christianity began "infecting" the world.

Until the thing became "endemic."

Every Christian knows he is "sent."

He knows he has a share in the mission of Jesus himself.

Who came "to set the earth on fire."

Francis Xavier understood this.

Mother Teresa of Calcutta understood this.

The thousands of missionaries—priests, sisters, religious brothers, lay missionaries—who are in mission lands understand this.

To this you are called.

No matter where you are—in your own country or abroad—you are sent, you are on a mission.

If you join the ranks of the priests or the religious you should know you are becoming an apostle by profession. Some people are accountants by profession.

Some doctors.

Street sweepers.

Engineers, drivers, cobblers, bank tellers.

You are an apostle of Jesus.

They are all apostles, but that is not what they do expressly most of the time.

You will be dedicated to the apostolate full time, to preach the Gospel. That will be your profession. To this you are called. To this you are sent.

This desire to spend oneself in spreading the Gospel is called *zeal*. Remember this word.

It's a key word to a priest or a religious.

An apostle must work for the Kingdom.

This zeal ought to eat him or her up.

And spur him or her to go out and preach.

Spread the Gospel.

It's a glorious thing, my friend.

To be associated with the mission of Jesus.

To build up his Church.

To this you are called.

It's a path in life not without hardships.

But it's a glorious mission in life.

Will you take it? ? ?

THE COST
PART ONE

Once when large crowds of people were going along with Jesus, he turned and said to them, "Whoever comes to me cannot be my disciple unless he loves me more than he loves his father and his mother, his wife and his children, his brothers and his sisters, and himself as well. Whoever does not carry his own cross and come after me cannot be my disciple. If one of you is planning to build a tower, he sits down first and figures out what it will cost, to see if he has enough money to finish the job. If he doesn't, he will not be able to finish the tower after laying the foundation; and all who see what happened will make fun of him. 'This man began to build but can't finish the job!' they will say.

"If a king goes out with ten thousand men to fight another king who comes against him with twenty thousand men, he will sit down first and decide if he is strong enough to face that other king. If he isn't, he will send messengers to meet the other king to ask for terms of peace while he is still a long way off. In the same way," concluded

Jesus, "none of you can be my disciple unless be gives up everything he has." (Luke 14:25–33)

Don't let these words scare you.

They're meant to sober down the overenthusiastic.

Besides, they're not said only to those who join the priesthood or religious life.

These words are addressed to all Christians, without distinction.

All Christians have to be ready to give Jesus full priority over anything dear to them.

All Christians—in whichever way of life they choose to follow Jesus—have a cross to carry.

Yet priests and religious have a specific cross to bear.

Don't get me wrong.

You can certainly find some unhappy priests.

And frustrated nuns, no doubt.

But by and large, the priestly and religious life is a happy life.

Those who have been called and who try to be faithful to their call live in joy and in peace.

Some crosses are heavy.

But, if carried with love, Jesus's cross doesn't have to be painful.

If carried with love—that is the catch phrase.

The cross of the religious is their lifestyle.

Specifically the three vows of religious life.

Poverty, chastity, obedience.

Their life is to be poor: **simple** life.

Trying to imitate the simplicity of the life Jesus, with his group of followers, led.

Some religious can become quite learned, famous, or influential. Yet they must keep themselves simple, unassuming.

Simplicity comes easy to the poor.

And then there is the vow of **celibacy.**

The priest and the religious give up the idea of building families of their own.

Theirs is a 100 percent dedication to the Kingdom. For the Kingdom the religious sacrifices a wife or a husband, children, posterity.

Actually celibacy is more than just giving up sex.

A married man wants posterity more than sex.

Every father secretly or overtly wants to perpetuate himself through his children.

He longs and tries to live on in them.

A woman naturally wants to become a mother.

A woman needs children to love.

To spend her tremendous capacity for love on someone who needs her totally, like a child.

Well, the priest and the religious do not exercise the natural expression of these very noble instincts.

They learn to transform and sublimate them into an intense apostolate, into serving and loving all with the greatness of the love of Jesus.

and in that way you'll "live on"—in your spiritual children!

And finally there is the vow of **obedience.**

When you join the priesthood or religious life, you also join an organized group, a team.

A family.

With a father or a mother running it.

In religious life the Superior interprets the will of God for the individual religious.

Or the bishop for his priests.

It is from them that the priest or religious receives his or her mission to preach the Good News.

The same way as the apostles received their mission from Jesus.

Yes, we talked about the life of the religious being a cross. These three vows are like three nails, rough and strong, that bind the religious to his or her cross.

Jesus's cross.

And that makes the life of the religious a continuous sacrifice.

For Jesus and for God's people.

A necessary one.

The religious thus proclaims in his or her life that Jesus and the Kingdom are all that matters to him or her.

Worldly values are not his or her values. He or she is not interested.

Saint Paul considered worldly values as rubbish.

Good to be dumped into a trashcan.

All Paul wanted to possess was Christ.

So does the priest.

So does the religious.

If this is what you, too, want,
If you're willing to imitate Jesus,
Who lived simply,
Who remained a celibate throughout his life,
Who always obeyed the will of his Father . . .

Well . . .

Now you know what it takes.
Jesus is trying to disabuse the impulsive.
He died on a cross.
(But he also rose up gloriously.)
Whoever means to follow Jesus sooner or later will have a meeting with his sidekick: Jesus's cross.
The religious, like everyone else, has his or her cross.
Perhaps the only difference is that in religious life, he or she finally learns to accept and love it.
And that makes the cross a sweet burden.

THE COST
PART TWO

Every year the parents of Jesus went to Jerusalem for the Passover Festival. When Jesus was twelve years old, they went to the festival as usual. When the festival was over they started back home, but the boy Jesus stayed in Jerusalem. His parents did not know this; they thought that he was with the group, so they traveled a whole day and then started looking for him among their relatives and friends. They did not find him, so they went back to Jerusalem looking for him. On the third day they found him in the Temple, sitting with the Jewish teachers, listening to them and asking questions. All who heard him were amazed at his intelligent answers. His parents were astonished when they saw him, and his mother said to him, "Son, why have you done this to us? Your father and I have been terribly worried trying to find you."

He answered them, "Why did you have to look for me? Didn't you know that I had to be in my Father's house?" But they did not understand his answer.

So Jesus went back with them to Nazareth where he was obedient to them. His mother treasured all these things in her heart. Jesus grew both in body and in wisdom, gaining favor with God and men. (Luke 2:41–52)

You can safely assume that the story of Samuel was a favorite with all boys in Israel.

Remember Samuel?

The boy who was called by God in a dream?

"Samuel, Samuel."

"Speak, Lord, for your servant is listening."

You can also assume that Jesus was familiar with this story.

He had heard it several times.

From his dad.

From his mom.

From his teacher.

At the synagogue services.

This story appealed to generous boys in Israel.

It appealed to the boy Jesus.

It also gave them ideas, at times funny ideas, as you have just read.

John the Baptist left his old parents, Zechariab and Elizabeth, and went to live with a religious community in the desert.

He was probably only twelve.

The boy Jesus decided to join the seminarians at the Temple.

He was twelve too.

Twelve-year-olds do bizarre things like these.

As you can see, at twelve Jesus simply acted his age.

He wanted to serve God.

He wanted to be like Samuel, who stayed in the Temple since childhood.

So, why not?

It was easy. He just slipped away and stayed behind.

His parents found him in the class of one of the famous professors of Scripture in Jerusalem. Lost among the group of seminarians.

And his parents did not like it.

Not what he did.

And much less the way he did it.

So, Mary scolded the boy.

And rightly so.

Like any other boy, Jesus at twelve, once in a while had to be called to order by his parents.

Jesus's reply to his parents came as a surprise.

"Why did you look for me? Didn't you know I am to be in my Father's house?"

Now, his parents' reaction is just as surprising.

"They did not understand."

And so they laid down the law and took him home.

Well done!

If you decide to follow Jesus's call, you'll have to count on your parents' reaction.

Will they understand what you're trying to do?

They might not.

Often, the love that parents have for their children blinds them.

Or at least it beclouds their reasoning powers.

At times they fear that a son or a daughter who leaves for the seminary or the convent is lost to them forever.

Or that their child is being duped by the priests or the sisters.

Or simply that he or she is too young to know what he or she is doing.

So, some parents don't want to hear about it. Or at least they resort to delaying tactics.

"Get a master's degree in economics first."

"A little work experience in the family business should help."

Anything to distract you from such a fantasy.

If this doesn't work, they might pluck the emotional chord.

"How can you do this to your parents?"

And the grandmother will readily agree.

And the auntie too.

And so on and so forth.

This might turn out to be the toughest hurdle you will have to clear in your quest to follow your call.

And the most painful of all.

For it will be a conflict between two most lofty loyalties.

Loyalty to God.

And loyalty to your parents and your family.

In theory, things are very clear: God demands to be given priority over all, parents included.

But in practice, the unrelenting pressure from the family and your own emotional attachment to it could become insurmountable.

And so, what are you going to do if your parents won't hear about it?

You're not going to "elope" with Jesus.

Twelve-year-old kids do that at times.

And they deserve a loving scolding.

Especially if you are still legally a minor, you'd better not try anything bizarre.

You've heard that prayer moves mountains, haven't you?

Quiet determination, too, has worn down the reluctance of many a parent.

After all, most parents want for their children what will make them happy in life.

Once they realize you mean business, they'll end up by yielding.

Willy-nilly, but they'll yield.

In this, your determination will be a decisive factor.

If you perceive God's call clearly and really want to follow Jesus permanently, you will never give up your quest.

It should not come as a surprise to you if your parents do not understand.

Zechariah and Elizabeth, the parents of John the Baptist, probably did not understand either.

Mr. Zebedee, the father of the Apostles James and John, did not understand when his two boys went away with Jesus and left him alone to do the fishing.

Joseph and Mary did not understand what the boy was telling them.

They understood only a few years later, when the man Jesus informed them he was taking himself to the roads, the villages, and the synagogues of Galilee to announce the arrival of the Kingdom.

Keep praying.

Someday your parents will finally understand what it is that you and God are trying to achieve in following your call.

JOHNNY . . .
WHAT'S HIS NAME?

As Jesus was starting on his way again, a man ran up, knelt before him, and asked him, "Good Teacher, what must I do to receive eternal life?"

"Why do you call me good?" Jesus asked him. "No one is good except God alone. You know the commandments: 'Do not commit murder; do not commit adultery; do not steal; do not accuse anyone falsely; do not cheat; respect your father and your mother.'"

"Teacher," the man said, "ever since I was young, I have obeyed all these commandments." Jesus looked straight at him with love and said, "You need only one thing. Go and sell all you have and give the money to the poor, and you will have riches in heaven; then come and follow me." When the man heard this, gloom spread over his face, and he went away sad, because be was very rich. (Mark 10:17–22)

You've read this story before, haven't you?

It's a sad story. No happy ending here.

It has a beautiful beginning. The ending is disappointing for all.

The young man was disappointed with Jesus's demands.

Jesus was disappointed with the young man's shilly-shallying.

We ourselves are all disappointed with the turn the story takes.

Here was a young man any dad would be proud to have as his junior.

A fine young man. Polite, wholesome, responsible, God-fearing.

Generous.

Or so he appeared.

He was not satisfied with himself. With everything he had done in life.

He hungered for more.

Is there still a challenge in life for me? he asked himself.

And then he happened to come into contact with Jesus.

He saw him at work. He heard him speaking. Inviting people to join the Kingdom, to be saved.

Did he recognize in Jesus something like the embodiment of what he wanted to be?

Did Jesus appear to him as his ideal personified?

He finally mustered all his courage.
And approached Jesus.

Oh, yes. He was not quite clear about what he wanted.
No young man ever really is.
So he just blurted out and echoed some of the words he had heard from Jesus's lips.
"Master, I want to be saved."

He also appeared to have a flair for the theatrical.
Most young people love drama.
He wouldn't come quietly, like old Nicodemus did, to sound Jesus out privately.
This young man made a big fuss about it.
He knelt down in front of the Master, spread his hands to him; his eyes shone with eagerness, his voice shook with the emotion of the most dramatic moment of his life.

Beneath all this fanfare, only one thing is worth noticing.
He finally managed to come face to face with the fascinating Master.
And would you believe it? It appears that he also fascinated Jesus.
For Jesus could be fascinated too.
By faith and generosity.
By the wit of a Canaanite woman.
By the faith of a Roman centurion.
By the eager prayer of a leper.

By an old lady coyly, yet in faith, touching the corner of his mantle.

Actually the young man's record was quite impressive.

Here was one who had been loyal to God all his life.

One who faithfully observed God's Law.

A true God-fearing Israelite.

A young man "according to the heart of God."

But loyalty, faithfulness, the fear of God were not enough for him.

Jesus felt he was ready to take the next step: the step from faithfulness to generosity.

Jesus decided to aim for the top. To call him to discipleship. To invite him to give all up and follow him.

The move failed.

And the thing blew up like a balloon pricked by a pin.

Something went very wrong.

Perhaps Jesus took a calculated risk. Perhaps he felt he had to. It was the next natural move. If there was anyone who appeared like an ideal disciple, it was he. It simply had to be tried.

Perhaps Jesus miscalculated the young man's wealth.

And his inordinate attachment to it.

The young man's face grew sad.

Still in that melodramatic kneeling position, he now felt confused, silly, ridiculous.

The drama was gone now. No more glamour. He stood up.

He did not even dare look at Jesus.

He shook the dust off his tunic at the knees. He fixed his fine linen girdle.

He turned around.

And he left, his mind blank, his heart wounded, and his dramatic enthusiasm drained.

———————

Do not ask for his name. No one knows it.

Sometimes history is kind enough not to record the name of cowards.

He had the chance of his life. He was invited to join the group of intimate friends of the Master.

To join the team.

He had what it took.

But he could not bring himself to pay the cost.

Was he able to live with that?

This young man's story could well be yours.

(Wow . . .)

A BUMPER CROP

The Kingdom of heaven is like this. Once there was a man who went out early in the morning to hire some men to work in his vineyard. He agreed to pay them the regular wage, a silver coin a day, and sent them to work in his vineyard. He went out again to the marketplace at nine o'clock and saw some men standing there doing nothing, so he told them, "You also go and work in the vineyard, and I will pay you a fair wage." So they went. Then at twelve o'clock and again at three o'clock he did the same thing. It was nearly five o'clock when he went to the marketplace and saw some other men still standing there. "Why are you wasting the whole day here doing nothing?" he asked them. "No one hired us," they answered. "Well, then, you go and work in the vineyard," he told them. (Matthew 20:1–7)

Because this parable was meant to illustrate an aspect of God's Kingdom, I think it reveals God's strategy to bring his Kingdom about.

Simply put, God's strategy appears to be this: Keep calling, never give up the search for more and more workers.

Again and again he goes out into the marketplace and hires people to work in his vineyard.

Some people feel the call early in life, some later on, some much later on.

There are early vocations and late vocations.

(Though I hope there are not retarded vocations!)

Keep calling, keep calling . . . someone will respond.

Who will?

In the parable, the unemployed, the idle responded.

In life, however, I don't think this is the case.

The idle won't respond.

The idle aren't equipped to hear the call, to begin with.

Much less to respond to it.

Most idle people don't have what it takes to follow Jesus.

Their lives are for the most part empty because their minds are mostly hollow.

Not fit for discipleship.

In fact, those who respond to Jesus's call are the busy ones.

Busy with the right things.

People who have their heads and their lives and their hearts filled with ideals, and dreams, and plans.

Jesus's call does not appeal to the small hearted, but to people who want to do something big in life.

And who, to earn it, are willing to sacrifice all else.

All—nothing excluded.

It could be your glory and your pride to work for Jesus.

To work with Jesus.

He's expecting a bumper crop and needs plenty of qualified harvesters: that is, generous harvesters.

Who are ready to work hard.

Ready to withstand the heat and the labor.

Ready to enjoy doing his work . . . the work of Jesus.

A great saint loved to say this prayer often:

Lord,
Teach me to be generous.
Teach me to serve you as you deserve;
To give and not to count the cost,
To fight and not to heed the wounds,
To toil and not to seek for rest,
To labor and not to ask for a reward,
Save that of knowing that I am doing your will.
Amen.

Ignatius of Loyola.

To this you are called.

Good luck to you.

BIBLICAL INDEX

		Pages
Matthew	2:1–12	38 39
	2:19–23	27
	5:13–16	102
	13:44–46	98
	20:1–7	125
	28:16–20	106
Mark	1:14–20	90
	1:40–45	56
	2:13–17	35
	3:13–15	22
	5:21–24	61 62
	5:35–42	61 62
	7:31–37	47
	10:17–22	120
	10:46–52	43 44
Luke	1:26–38	18 19
	2:41–52	114 115
	10:38–42	84
	14:25–33	109 110
	19:1–10	79
John	1:35–42	94
	1:43–51	31 32
	4:1–26	51 53
	6:1–15	12 13
	11:1–44	65 68
Acts	9:1–19	73 74